-1|4

Janet Boulton

FOREGROUND
BACKGROUND

About Making a Garden

2013

To the memory of my Mother and Father

ISBN 978–0–9568559–1–6
Copyright © 2013 Janet Boulton
Designed and produced by Colin Sackett
Distributed by uniformbooks.co.uk

Contents

Introduction

When I began to garden here in Abingdon, Oxfordshire at the beginning of the 1980s I had no particular ideas other than making borders for flowers and shrubs, getting in a few trees and having a path with a patch of grass somewhere.

This long narrow plot (6m x 34.5m) behind a tall terraced house of no architectural distinction had been unfenced and neglected for years. Apart from the ash and sycamore trees belonging to my neighbours overshadowing the far end, there was nothing to inspire nor to save.

It may have been that had I known something about small garden design and been without financial limitations, I would have enclosed it with proper walls and divided the space into the so-called rooms that were in vogue at that time. As it was, I resorted to laplarch fencing two metres high, got rid of the grass and made a winding path between what is in effect two borders.

The winding path has two virtues. First, it slows down progress through the garden, making it seem bigger and giving a more varied spacial experience. Secondly, being flexible by having no hard edges (built up over the years of impacted local peagrit), it is possible to plant into it and change the contours a little depending on circumstances. It also increases the chance of self-seeding, and is soft and unfocused. The fence, now well-covered in a variety of ivies, is kept neat by being treated like a vertical lawn.

Reading and bookbuying were essential to my learning more about gardening, garden history, and design. *Popular Gardening* magazine was a colourful and fruitful weekly source of good sense and instruction in all the seasonal activities of the gardening year. Also the advertisements introduced me to all manner of products and sidelines. It was probably through these columns that I got into the pleasures of buying secondhand books by post from a number of garden book dealers. In their seductive catalogues I found out about the history of garden publishing and its specialisms and factions. To mention a few: the publications of Gertrude Jekyll, Dawn Macleod and Margery Fish, histories of Italian gardens, herbals, plant collecting, illustrated books, biographies and autobiographies of gardeners and designers of the past. Today, libraries and bookshops have shelves filled with books on every conceivable aspect of the garden world but in the late seventies there was little readily available and certainly no garden design schools or luscious TV programmes.

Plant-buying must rate high on the list of pleasures for any gardener. In the early days here in Abingdon there was Tesco Garden Centre (opened with great ceremony by the early TV gardener, Percy Thrower). Hellmans Nurseries had a stall selling shrubs at the Monday market. Nearby in the village of Longworth was the enchanting P-J Nursery selling the rarer perennials and trees. It was Elizabeth Parker-Jervis who recommended I went to see Anne Dexter's garden in North Oxford because in a situation almost identical to mine, she had established a much-admired plantlovers' garden. Alas, all these people and nurseries no longer exist, and apart from a few pleasurable excursions further afield, I now tend to buy most plants in the local garden centres—Millett's Farm, B&Q, and Homebase. All three often stock, alongside the staple favourites, many of the less common varieties which not so long ago could be bought only at a specialist nursery.

I painted Anne Dexter's garden at Beech Croft Road, Oxford and indeed all the gardens I have subsequently made paintings of, mostly as a means toward learning as much as possible about what it is that goes into the making and maintaining of a beautiful garden. I seem to have spent as much time mooning about and photographing as sitting in front of an easel. Looking intently at 50-odd varieties of clematis, noticing the various supports and plants, the miniature shade garden at the end by the false door, stuffed with treasures, the alpine collection near the house, meticulously labelled —all gave me an insight into the world of the passionate plant collector and the artistry needed to make it all into a garden rather than a museum. Also it convinced me that it is possible to make something worthwhile in a small, unpromising space.

By 1984 I had begun to paint at Barnsley House, near Cirencester. Here Rosemary and David Verey had made a rather grander garden which along with an interest in plants contained many of the features characteristic of the Edwardian Arts and Crafts Movement. These formal elements—temples, allées, knot gardens, yew

Barnsley House Herb Garden *1990*

hedging and topiary, sculpture and water features—added an architectural dimension to the world of the plant specialist, whose gardens are for the most part less structured. My particular fascination was with the kitchen garden—a modest potager on the edge of a field with brick paths edged with boxwood defining a symmetrical design of rectangular beds containing all manner of fruit trees and vegetables—both functional and decorative. This garden, with its use of evergreen on a small scale, inspired me to put more structure into the garden here. The Q parterre behind the studio, the ivy arch leading to the willow tree and the boxwood topiary in the borders were all introduced at about this time.

It is inevitable that anyone interested in the history and design of gardens would want to visit the gardens in Italy. Up to the year 2000 I made innumerable painting trips, sometimes in the late autumn and winter months, generally to Florence but twice to Rome. During all these years I spent most time at the Villa La Pietra. When it was not convenient for Sir Harold Acton to have me, I went into the Boboli Gardens attached to the Palazzo Pitti. Here, at the far end near the Porto Romano, I concentrated on the 16th-century Isolotto centred on the great Gianbologna Fountain.

The cumulative effect of spending so much time drawing, painting and photographing in these great classical gardens, whose structure and meaning remain constant throughout the year, has been to convince me of the value of light and form, and how much all-round interest and gravitas they bring to even the most restricted domain.

Oceanus Fountain, Isolotto, Boboli Gardens
August 1990

Irish Yews, entrance to the middle of the garden

Villa La Pietra, Pots with Ceres and Diana *1990*

Gaining in confidence, I planted six Irish yews, four of which are paired, beside the short path leading from the busy street to my front door. The other two, either side of the winding path, mark the entrance to the middle part of the garden at the back. The two metre square of dwarf boxwood beyond a rectangular paved area at the top of the steps, and the inclusion of a greater variety of evergreen shrubs—lonicera, laurel, holly, bay, yew, griselina, euonymous—can all be attributed to my time in Italy.

By the time I had acquired twenty or so pots there was a suggestion of my 'getting over-potted'. Now that there are four times that number it doesn't seem to matter. Again this was due to the influence of Italy in that the gardens there contain dozens of pots—all of terracotta and all employed to some purpose. Here, keeping it simple, buying them unadorned in sets of differing sizes and then placing them in groups, they are somehow absorbed. Even though most pots are guaranteed frost-hardy these days, at the end of each year they are carefully wrapped and stored. Many of them are irreplaceable, such as the early Jim Keeling pots from Whichford Pottery, and a set of twenty bought from Rosemary Verey (these were specially made with large holes in their sides for an old nurseryman specialising in boxwood). There are also four large pots standing on brick plinths outside the studio, with smaller matching ones beside them containing ferns—a bargain buy from Tesco.

There are other things/accoutrements in the garden acquired about twenty years ago which have stood the

test of time and sentiment. These include half a dozen iron plant supports designed by Margery Fish and made by the local blacksmith for her iconic cottage garden at East Lambrook Manor in Somerset; a seat by Charles Verey which in summer is flanked by the more plebeian tomato and bean plants; a cast-iron sewing machine stand tucked away behind the tool shed; and a zinc well bucket containing bamboo canes, as well as a miscellany of chimney pots—affordable sculpture!

By 1990 the overall shape and form of the garden seemed to have settled down and acquired an air of maturity. At the same time I had begun to lose interest in trying to maintain a garden full of interesting and unusual plants. I was losing too many of the plants, and worrying and shopping too often. Thus, the amateur learns? I resolved to simplify and concentrate on plants best suited to the shaded space that had evolved, such as ferns, clematis and hardy geraniums and to restrict any irresistable treasures and impulse buys to containers. In fact, I did think of doing something entirely different. One thought, the shape of the garden suggested it, was to make an allotment with a greenhouse, sheds and a few hens.

However, in July 1993 I made a long-anticipated visit to Little Sparta—the garden made by Ian and Sue Finlay up in the Pentland Hills, due south of Edinburgh. It was here I began to consider the possibilities of having a garden that contained more than plants. In a radio interview Ian Hamilton Finlay had said it was quite possible for a gardener to make a work reflecting his ideas. He suggested

ABOVE: Common enchanters nightshade with clematis. BELOW: Lords and ladies with fern.

planting a 'wee grove of trees' and placing a plaque inscribed with the name of someone/something loved therein.

Art, the history and practice of gardening, and the human spirit are the sources of inspiration behind the works in the garden here. It is slowly developing as ideas come and the means to realise them are available. The use of inscriptions and epigrams is an ancient practice but at Little Sparta Ian Hamilton Finlay took it to a new level, making a contemporary interpretation of a classical idea. Although most of the works here are indicative of my own interests, they owe everything to his mode of expression. The sixteen years spent painting in Scotland culminated in an exhibition 'Remembering Little Sparta' (The Sculpture Court, ECA, Edinburgh Festival, 2009). It marked the end of that period.

In October 2010 having decided to stop travelling to paint, I was lucky to get permission from the Cow Mead Allotment Association in Oxford to be a visiting artist, thus fulfilling a long-cherished idea. My objective was to make a study of the allotment, perhaps in the end amounting to a record, but of course it is a perfect opportunity to see just how things are done in this highly individualistic kind of horticulture. The influence of making frequent trips into Oxford and spending more time in my own garden has inspired works relating to 'grow your own' and self-sufficiency. Buying my first shed, learning to grow vegetables, soft fruit and herbs in pots, incorporating more cottage plants from seed and leaving all the wild plants are manifestations of a new direction.

Little Sparta, Apollo & Daphne *1996*

The shed with a quote from Voltaire's *Candide*: "After all, the best thing we can do is cultivate our garden".

Common bindweed, golden hop and holly.

Last year there was an abundance of common enchanter's nightshade and herb robert in the borders, bryony festooned the wild holly, and hedge bindweed competed with the golden hop on the back fence.

As for help in the garden, the tree surgeon comes annually to tame the willow and azara, as well as thinning the rhamnus. (None these plants would have been introduced by a trained designer into a garden this size). Otherwise, Dilys Fleet has been coming for twenty years to keep the garden in order—she manages to make a few hours seem worth a week.

It is good to know that the flexibility in this garden has allowed me to move in another direction with not too much trouble or expense.

It may be that some time in the future those early crazes for 'must-have' plants and collecting will return, perhaps a passion for cacti or succulents… who knows?

Background

Growing up on a farm and having a father who was that
rare thing, a keen naturalist and gardener as well as a farmer,
was a good beginning. Living in North Wiltshire on the
edge of the Cotswolds where the Arts and Crafts Movement
flourished, houses and gardens associated with that style
were very familiar. As it happened, in Stanton Fitzwarren,
our nearest village, the 'big house' garden was reputed to have
been designed by Gertrude Jekyll, albeit one of the many she
did by post. The walled kitchen garden was fully functional
in the traditional way with its head gardener, garden boys
and hothouses. Beyond in the pleasure garden there were
fine cedars, clipped yew hedging and topiary, and a prized
all-blue herbaceous border which culminated in stone steps
leading up toward the house. This was surrounded by a wide
swathe of lawn ending in a ha-ha, meadows, small lake and
woodland. Amongst the trees stood the reconstructed west
end of St Leonard's Church (dismantled by the Victorians)
which served as an eyecatcher.

So, in this small community of 250 or so souls I became
familiar with not only all the rich variety of cottage and
farmhouse gardens with their vegetable plots, cinder paths,
rabbit hutches, bird baths, rockeries and the odd quirky
summerhouse, but also a modest example of an arts and
crafts garden attached to what seemed to be remnant of an
18th-century landscape.

Nearby Swindon was rich in allotment sites, some of
which could be seen to advantage on my way to school
on the little branch line train connecting the village to the

Going for a picnic, 6th August 1945

My father, with sweet peas and chrysanthemums, 1966

centre of town. Up the hill in the Old Town were the Town Gardens, a fine example of Victorian garden design. Daily walks in crocodile led through the wrought iron gates and along winding paths bordered with evergreen shrubs. There was a scented garden for the blind, a meticulously labelled formal rose garden, an aviary, and a bandstand. Expansive lawns were dotted with specimen trees and a few large island beds with seasonal annuals set out in those formal patterns beloved of this kind of municipal garden.

In contrast, in 1950 the twelve-acre Queen's Garden was opened in the New Town. Commemorating those who fought in the Second World War, it was constructed around a disused quarry and set out to be naturalistic and attractive to wildlife.

Towards the end of my schooldays we were taken to the 1951 Festival of Britain. Here I had my first experience of seeing a Modernist garden which was sophisticated and urban. This garden was designed by H. F. Clarke and Maria Shepheard. Its most striking feature was the deliberate use of architectural plants around a pool edged with pebbles and boulders, with that ectoplasmic shape so often to be seen in surrealist paintings. A Lynn Chadwick sculpture with controlled flowing lines in green bronze adorned the grass area.

The intervening twenty-five or so years from the end of my youth and coming to Abingdon were largely taken up with my life as a painter and teacher, and later on with family preoccupations.

Painting the Gardens

Watercolour is known as a good medium for painting *en plein air*. Its characteristic luminosity and fluidity are perfect for expressing the transitory behaviour of weather and light. It is decisive and immediate as well as being quick to dry and relatively easy to transport. Paul Cézanne's landscapes in watercolour were a particular inspiration to me, not only because of his deployment of pencil as an integral part of the process of making a picture but also his objective way of using small areas of transparent pigment. Of course there are technical considerations and restraints wherever one paints, the worst of these being rain or a high moisture content in the atmosphere which causes the paper to buckle and be unresponsive to pencil and paint.

At Little Sparta in the Pentland Hills, with its upland pastures and moorland, high winds meant staking the easel into the ground or securing it to a tree. I did on occasion experience ice forming on the paper, and a frozen brush. Perversely, the light in autumn or winter was often more sympathetic than in high summer, when it rained more and the greens were dominant and heavy. In Italy, the intense heat meant finding good solid shade which lasted for an hour or two before the sun moved round. The blinding light on the white paper meant that the easel and board must also be in shadow, as well as free of the dappled effect of light through trees. The early 17th-century Isolotto in the Boboli Gardens, designed by Alphonso Parigi, is a perfect place for an artist. It comprises an oval-shaped enclave bounded by a very tall hedge, set into which are a number of arbours,

Bobili Gardens, Perseus *1989*

Little Sparta, The Present Order II *2000*

Villa La Pietra, The Kitchen Garden, Lemon Trees *1991*

20

each containing a broad stone seat facing the beautiful island with its central Oceanus Fountain by Gianbologna. Here I could accommodate myself and my gear, as well as being able to move round all day long following the shade. The only irritants were the odd roving mosquito or a cloud of midges.

Up in the hills outside Florence, the nine-acre garden at the Villa La Pietra was also very amenable to being painted. Perhaps this was because its creator, Arthur M. Acton (1873–1953), was a painter as well as a garden maker and art collector. It has a seemingly inexhaustible range of vistas, terraces and statuary, all interrelated in a succession of perfect compositions. The main consideration here was not getting in the way or spoiling the view.

Staying in central Florence, my half hour walk across town in the early morning, to the Palazzo Pitti and up into the Boboli Gardens, made a pleasant start to the day. Catching the erratic number 25 bus from beside the Duomo up to La Pietra, with all my equipment and supplies, was more arduous. Fortunately, it was possible to stay all day, because I had access to the 17th-century Limonaia which formed part of the walled kitchen garden attached to the side of the villa. Apart from acting as a store for the pots of lemon trees in winter, it also functioned as garden shed, bothy and repository for a number of large wooden statues, antique pots and ancient carts. Here I could take refuge from the heat at siesta time and make paintings of other aspects of life in the garden.

The same good fortune followed me to Little Sparta. As a guest at Stonypath (the croft which was the Finlay home attached to the garden), I became known as the 'sometimes-

Villa La Pietra, Limonaia, Vanity & Abundance *1991*

resident-artist'. Here, continuing my practice of working on quite a large scale, I aimed to make works which were completed *in situ*. This would have been quite impractical had permission not been given to occupy the Temple to Apollo. This converted farm building also acted, at this time, as a store for Ian Hamilton Finlay's sculpture. Inside, along with the original wall plaques and classical figures in white plaster, there were wheelbarrows, bronze watering cans and wellies, stone beehives and inscribed garden tools—a treasure house of fascinating things awaiting exhibition. So out of the bad weather and seemingly by chance, it was made possible to study a subject uncannily, wondrously similar to that of the Limonaia at Villa La Pietra, thus giving me an insight into the ethos of this other more contemporary 20th-century neo-classical garden.

At the Cow Mead Allotments in Oxford, I travelled by bus from Abingdon, alighting at a stop just opposite. It had been agreed with the allotment committee that I would pay my dues like any other allotmenter and likewise have use of the code to open the gates. Cow Mead is a rectangular site dating back to the First World War (at least). There are 140 plots, laid out in four parallel rows divided by two fine wide grass tracks to allow vehicle access. It is surrounded on two sides by 1930s and 1950s housing and a busy road, while the other sides overlook a small farm, meadows and the river Thames.

As with the potager at Barnsley House, Gloucestershire, the Beth Chatto Nursery, Essex, and the classical gardens of Italy, it is the geometric layout and repetition in the planting that attracts me to allotments, and within this framework the contrasts of individual expression personal to each owner.

Little Sparta, Temple to Apollo, Aphrodite with Beehive *2007*

Cow Mead Allotments, Sheds *2012*

I wonder if an allotment might be seen as akin to a bed in a hospital ward—a personal space within an ordered public domain. It took me well over a year to lose the sense of being intrusive . Eventually I was able to sit and make small paintings by getting to know more people and asking their permission. It was a help to say that I was making a kind of record. The exceptionally poor weather was a great hindrance in 2012, but unlike those large roomy refuges from sun and storm at Little Sparta and Villa La Pietra, there would have been, even if invited, no room for me and my easel in any of the exceptionally diverse sheds to be found at Cow Mead. Nevertheless, I was given an number of opportunities to make quick drawings and take photographs of some fascinating, expressive interiors . Although differing in many ways from the other grander examples of garden-related buildings, they have the same purpose and beauty, with their wheelbarrows, tools, seed packets, kettles, chairs and accumulations of garden detritus, and in one instance some decorative butterflies and whimsical figures attached to the ceiling.

Photography

Being amateur and free of restrictions, using a camera in the gardens has been most enjoyable. I have unintentionally amassed quite extensive collections of photographs, albeit unstructured and personal, of the Villa La Pietra, the Isolotto, Little Sparta and the Cow Mead Allotments. At times it has been possible to record something unusual:a fleeting effect,

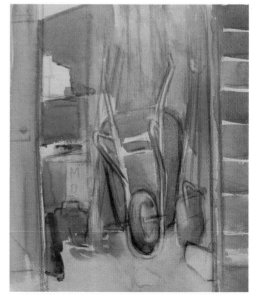

Cow Mead Allotments, Shed with Wheelbarrow
2012

'Remembering Little Sparta'
The Sculpture Court, Edinburgh College of Art,
Edinburgh Festival, 2009

a temporary event or the glimpse of an interior rarely seen.

Photographing in the winter months, when the gardens are stripped of their finery, has been essential to a better understanding of the true nature of the place. Having a clearer idea of the terrain, its linear design and shape in the wider environment, and seeing the way plants connect to the ground and one another, all contribute to gaining a stronger sense of being at one with the whole.

Any success I have had with photographing my own garden is due to spending so much time here that I am, on occasion, able to catch that once-only moment when details look at their finest.

The only solo show of my garden paintings in London ('Two Gardens', Redfern Gallery, Cork Street, w1. 2001) was mostly made up of paintings 'en plein air' in Italy and Scotland. I first began to use photographs extensively towards the end of my time at Little Sparta. In 2006, as Resident Artist at the Edinburgh College of Art, with a spacious studio, I was able to review the numerous unfinished paintings, sketches and notes made since my first visit in 1993. With the additional help of photography it was possible to complete a new series.

I shall always be ambivalent about using a photograph as an *aide-memoire*. It is a bewildering and somehow contradictory discipline to add to the process of making an image. While often reassuring, it can complicate perception by interfering with true memory and spontaneous response.

The Garden Works

Making these works has been a relatively new venture. Hitherto, the nearest I have come to doing anything sculptural has been constructing paper reliefs made with paper pulp.

The design and planting of the garden was established by the early 1990s and I have not needed to make any appreciable alterations to accommodate the works. It seems as if the spaces and plants have themselves prompted certain thoughts: such as FLIGHT in a sunless part of the border or RIVER-BANK under the willow tree. It may also be that as a painter of still life, composing with objects in a given space is second nature.

In preparing this part of the text, I have come to realise that long before I came under the spell of Ian Hamilton Finlay and Little Sparta, I already had a lifelong interest in Cubist Art and its influence. This relates in particular those still life paintings in which words, signs and encoded messages are an integral part of their meaning. Poetry, language and letterforms have always been important. Moreover, all the works in the garden are designed and positioned to be seen and read from one side. Thus they retain the two-dimensional characteristic of a painting, a page or a work in relief. Amongst my most favourite pictures are those which connect the objects to something in Nature, as in the paintings of Georges Braque, Juan Gris and Paul Nash, when the still life is interacting with a scene beyond the window. Perhaps the installations in the garden here could be understood in the same spirit: that is when equal value is given to the object and the place.

Key to the works on p.36–37

18

24 | 32   26 | 25

Glass—windows, mirrors, glass objects standing on or in front of reflective surfaces, assembled on long shelves or placed on tables—forms in one way or another the most persistent subject of my still life pictures.

This fascination with glass and its potential is used in three ways. Firstly, I use window panes to support words: JARDIN and ILLI QUINQUE GRADUS on the doors leading into the garden, and BRAQUE/BARQUE/BAROQUE on the studio windows.

Secondly, freestanding: LAWN, a sandblasted pane attached to the garden gate; NATURE MORTE, two parallel panes set into slate on a brick plinth; POÉSIE and PSYCHÉ, a matching pair placed on stone plinths reflecting each other across the garden path; and FLOWER SHOW, AMULANDO SOLVITUR? and WORK IN PROGRESS, using blue glass.

Lastly, by placing a pane of glass horizontally to protect the slate surface of the inscriptions in QUINQUNX and IN MEMORIAM it also serves to reflect the sky and trees. In RIVER-BANK the glass is sandblasted with the letters -XO and rests on a slate surface scored with squares seen diagonally. GNOS, made in white neon, must also be included in this category.

The use of glass as a material works well in a garden of this size. It excludes and blocks nothing since it is both clear and discrete, and it brings another dimension by refracting and reflecting wider spaces and including the sky, as well as lightening the tendency to darkness. Glass has some of the attributes of water with its reflectiveness, its clarity and its flatness, and since I have not yet found a way of introducing water into the garden, it serves as a fair substitute.

11

ambulando solvitur ?

17

6 | 2

Wood is another material used: oak for POSTCODE, cherry for HEARTH and LIVE UNKNOWN, mostly plywood for GARDEN CUPBOARD and pine for UMBRAUMBRAE. Two blocks of Serbian oak (a gift from a friend) are used as display stands. Half a dozen plinths supporting terracotta pots are in red brick for simplicity. Grey industrial brick is used for RIVER-BANK and NATURE MORTE, a more appropriate colour for these works.

Slate accords so well with Victorian red brick with its beautiful colour, especially in the rain. A number of works have been made from a defunct billiards table: FLIGHT, IN MEMORIAM and QUINQUNX came out of this, and it has also been used for the surfaces of TRIBUTE TO JUAN GRIS, RIVER-BANK and FAITH.

There are a number of works using perspex and acrylic lettering, including the ALLOTMENT HOLDER, HORIZON, IL FAUT CULTIVER NOTRE JARDIN, LES DEMOISELLES D'ABINGDON, NORD-SUD and POMA AMORIS. I think some of these would translate well into more enduring materials but on the other hand I like their bright, makeshift qualities and they are cheap and easy to maintain. TRIBUTE TO PAUL NASH and ATTENZIONE! comprise birds' nests, both of which are woven with durable plastic-coated electrical wiring in various colours.

3 | 13

7 | 33

29 | 22

14 | 27

9 | 10

20 | 4

21 | 5

35

A Key to the Garden & Notes on the Works

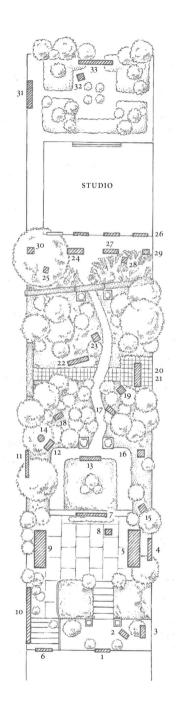

STUDIO

1. JARDIN
Door to garden.

2. WORK IN PROGRESS
A garden is never finished.

3. GARDEN CUPBOARD
A toy greenhouse and/or a shed.

4. THE ALLOTMENT HOLDER
A vertical allotment.

5. BASKET
To Colin Sackett and his use of words.

6. ILLI QUINQUE GRADUS
Those (well known) five steps. Also a reference to the first five steps of the 'Twelve-Step Recovery Programme'.

7. LIVE UNKNOWN
From Epicurus—an injunction for modesty. An idea borrowed from Ian Hamilton Finlay with his approval.

8. CHAMOMILE LAWN
Nostalgia.

9. HOMAGE TO JUAN GRIS
A still life on a table of slightly exaggerated proportions (implying an altar). Ivy, brick, stone: the whole work made in limited colours characteristic of the analytical period of early Cubist art. His sumptuous yet restrained use of white is represented in the graphic devices depicting his dates, the white flowers and the labels. Many of the characteristics in my paintings are contained in this work.

10. UMBRAUMBRAE
Shade of shades. Expressive of the importance of tone and the presence of shadow, foreboding. Using the elongated horizontal favoured in many of my still life paintings and paper reliefs.

Box Square

11. HORIZON
A three-metre horizontal with lettering derived from INFINITE/INFINITY/NON FINITO. The words YEN and YON are made in clear perspex to distinguish them from the blue of the other letters. A work evoking the experience of looking at a panorama: placed below eye level in a dark part of the garden.

12. FAITH
Back to front, reflected—not easy.

13. LES DESMOISELLES D'ABINGDON
A lighthearted work drawing on the title of Picasso's seminal Cubist painting 'Les Demoiselles D'Avignon' from 1908. The common names of cottage garden flowers.

15

14. TRIBUTE TO PAUL NASH
The plaque is based on an early PN logo. He referred to the joys of birds nesting in a letter to his girlfriend in 1910 (cf. *Dear Mercia, Paul Nash letters to Mercia Oakley, 1909–1918* ed. Janet Boulton).

15. THIS IS NOT AN ATTACK
In one of IHF's *Detached Sentences on Gardening* he writes "Certain gardens are described as retreats when they are really attacks". A humorous piece where the spouts of the watering cans could be seen as either trumpets or guns.

16. NATURE MORTE
Expressing the simultaneous all-round treatment of form and space in Cubist art. The lettering on glass from opposite sides, the whole space represented using reflection and transparency, and including the viewer.

Winding Path

17. AMBULANDO SOLVITUR?
Possibly resolve problem by taking a walk.

18. FLIGHT
In a dark part of the garden. Aspiration.

19. PSYCHÉ
Reflecting Poésie across the garden. A French word also meaning a mirror—depiction of bevill-edged mirror.

20. FLOWER SHOW
Flower show. Nostalgia. Celebrating a village event.

21. AMORIS POMA
Love apples.

22. HEARTH
Placed at the centre of the garden. Hear. Heart. Earth. Art.

23. POÉSIE
George Braque said "Poésie is the quality I admire above all else in art"—depiction of a picture frame.

Shade Area

24. RIVER-BANK
The River Ock is nearby, the willow and sky are reflected as in water. Also refers to my use of chequers and words in still life paintings and relief works.

25. GNOS
Tree of Knowledge. Song.

26. BRAQUE/BARQUE/BAROQUE
On the studio windows, using George Braque's preferred colours, a reference to his love of boats and the sensuous richness of his work.

27. NORD—SUD
A sign post. Title of short-lived journal published by the poet Pierre Reverdy—an admirer of Cubist artists he said "They lie less".

28. IN MEMORIAM
An old apple picking ladder. A dedication to all lost orchards and my own lost apple tree.

29. ATTENZIONE!
A scrape with two eggs. Nostalgia. An Admonition. A warning.

30. LAWN
Nostalgia. Aspiration.

Parterre

31. IL FAUT CULTIVER NOTRE JARDIN
A quote from *Candide*. Voltaire's summing up "After all, the best thing we can do is cultivate our garden".

32. Q
Quinqunx. An ancient Persian garden design.

33. ML11 8NG
Postcode for Little Sparta —a reminder and an acknowledgement.

12

Medlars *1985*

Garden Literature & the Illustrated Book

It is hard to see the wood for the trees when it come to thinking about other influences. For instance, being a booklover, many of my garden-related acquisitions have been acquired for their own sake and collected in an opportunist and unstructured way. I bought Chris Baines's *Making a Wildlife Garden* after seeing his stand at the Chelsea Flower Show in 1985, yet at the same time introducing a boxwood parterre and other formal elements into the garden here.

Nevertheless looking back over more than thirty years, there are a number of books which were revelations. They contributed greatly to my understanding of the making of gardens and the kinds of people who were, one way or another, passionate about gardens and gardening. Early on, my search for painters specialising in garden subjects led me to the work of the artist/gardener Margaret Waterfield (1860–1950) and her *Flower Groupings in English, Scotch and Irish Gardens* [1]. Her knowledge of plants and her bold expressive watercolours make her unique among that school of garden painters as described in *Painted Gardens 1860–1914* by P. Hobhouse and C. Wood [2]. In this category a favourite acquisition is a very handsome publication entitled *Some English Gardens* [3], which contains fifty examples of George S. Elgood's carefully composed watercolours. These demonstrate his skill in depicting the contrast of clipped yew combined with herbaceous borders in their full glory. I was intrigued by two books which demonstrate the existence of 'factions' in garden philosophy in the late Victorian period: *The Formal Garden* [4] by Reginald Blomfield and William Robinson's *The Wild Garden* [5] with delightful engravings by

1. J M Dent & Company, 1907
2. Pavilion Books, 1988
3. Longmans Green and Co., 1904
4. Macmillan & Co., 1892
5. John Murray, 3rd edition, 1883

Alfred Parsons. Books containing botanical illustrations rather than photographs of plants have a strong appeal. The painter/plantsman John Nash's (1893–1977) spiky modernist studies have an individualism and energy that enliven the many books he illustrated, *Poisonous Plants* [6], being especially covetable. The work of Stella Ross-Craig, seen in her *Drawings of British Plants made at Kew* [7], is the supreme example of the contemporary illustrator showing a rigorous sensibility within the constraints of a scientific discipline.

Fine old books telling of gardens long since gone or of those in their earlier existence often tell a lasting truth. I once glimpsed in Daniel Lloyd's bookshop in Mortlake Terrace, Kew, a very battered edition of Ellen Willmott's *Warley Place*. Surely, no garden restoration could ever replicate the scale and intensity of her legendary, ruinous obsession with plants, as seen in these pre-WWI sepia photographs? *The Gardens of Italy* [8] contains dozens of masterly works by the great Charles Latham, 1847–1912. Today, a hundred years later, the experience of being in these gardens (often necessarily restored) is greatly enhanced by having absorbed his record of the textures and tones of a bygone era. Ronald Blythe's recent classic, *Outsiders: A Book of Garden Friends* [9], is richly illustrated and celebrates the work of the more contemporary photographer, Edwin Smith (1912–1971) in black and white. In the same way, without the often restless impressionistic effect of unedited colour photography, his depiction of the cottage garden achieves a classical stillness and gravity—nostalgic yet not sentimental.

My first introduction to a garden that owes something to Cubist art was in *Gardens in the Modern Landscape* [10].

Plums *1985*

Irish Mollie *1985*

6. The Bodley Head, 1927
7. G. Bell & Sons, 1950s
8. Country Life Books, 1904
9. Black Dog Books, 2008
10. The Architectural Press, 1938
11. The Architectural Press, 1953
12. Reaktion Books, 1985
13. London Magazine Editions, 1967
14. Frances Lincoln, 2003
15. Polygon, 1995
16. Wild Hawthorn Press, 2004

Here Christopher Tunnard includes a photograph of a compact garden in Hyeres, wedged on a narrow terrace overlooking a vast landscape. Designed by Gabriel Guvrekian, it is a triangle at whose steep apex a dark sculpture by Lipschitz is placed on a plinth. The raised, chequered flower beds with their symmetrical planting, and the bright overall clarity of the design, are exciting because they connect the garden to other innovations in the world of the arts, without abjuring the use of plants. Another seminal book on this subject is Peter Shepheard's *Modern Gardens* [11] which show the best examples of garden design in Europe and the USA—scarcely rivalled to this day.

In 1987 at the Whitechapel Gallery Bookshop, I bought Yves Abrioux's study of the work of Ian Hamilton Finlay at Little Sparta, entitled *A Visual Primer* [12]. Tucked away in this densely informative book are some illustrations by the fine watercolourist, Ian Gardner, which depict Albert Speer's garden in Spandau Prison. These small paintings, with their limited palette of green and red, display an expressive minimalism characteristic of Speer's garden.

When at last in 1993 I visited Little Sparta, it was the beginning of a sixteen-year association. During this period I read widely on subjects associated with and about Ian Hamilton Finlay. These included *Concrete Poetry*, a fascinating international anthology (out of print) by Stephen Bann [13] and Jessie Sheeler's *Little Sparta* illustrated with strong colour photography by Andrew Lawson [14] which gives a sensitive and comprehensive account of a complex subject. *Wood Notes Wild* [15], edited by Alec Finlay, is a revelatory collection of essays on his art and poetry, while *Fleur De L'Air* [16], the name of a thirty acre garden in Provence designed by Ian Hamilton Finlay, is a handsome publication with moody tonal photography by Volkmar Herre, accompanied by brilliant, erudite commentaries by the poet Harry Gilonis.

Prior to this, my reading on the history of the landscape garden came through Dorothy Stroud's beautiful publication *Capability Brown* [17], and John Dixon Hunt's *Garden and Grove* [18]. Going round the Leazowes (and the golf course) on a rainy day, armed with R. Dodsley's account of William Shenstone's 'Ferme Ornee' at Halesowen [19], is a memorable and engaging experience. Reading a recent history by Jane Brown, *My Darling Heriott* [20] where she weaves an evocative account of an 18th-century gardener whose work scarcely exists, is another example of how it is possible to engage with something whose most vital existence is in prose. Now, in a similar spirit I am looking forward to visiting the gardens of Japan, inexpensively and in comfort, through the pages of a well-documented book of black and white photographs.

Presently self-sufficiency and wildness have come to the fore, as exemplified by growing produce in containers and letting self-seeded plants have their way. Apart from reading *The Allotment: it's landscape and culture* by David Crouch and Colin Ward [21], Jeremy Burchardt's *The Allotment Movement in England 1793–1873* [22] (both essential histories), and about the phenomenon of the community gardens springing up in major cities all over the world, I have found myself reading in the wider context of other more recent observations on the garden and the landscape. This includes Robert Pogue Harrison's *Gardens: an essay on the human condition* [23], *Arcadia revisited: the place of landscape* [24],

ABOVE:
Little Sparta, The Roman Garden: Nautilus
paper relief, 2007
BELOW:
Little Sparta, The Roman Garden: Carrier Stacks
paper relief collage, 2005

OPPOSITE PAGE:
Cow Mead Allotments, Winter
paper relief with acrylic, 2011

with its essay by Richard Mabey entitled 'Wildness as an Aesthetic Quality', and *Anticipatory history* [25], a discussion connecting past, present and future environmental change.

In the beginning I read all the popular weeklies, and I'm doing this again now, as well as subscribing to the monthly and quarterly journals published by the many societies. David Wheeler's *Hortus* and Patrick Eyres' *New Arcadian Journal*, privately published and long-established, are both firmly kept on the bookshelves, being full of fine writing and original illustrations. This is true too of the catalogues of some booksellers and specialist nurseries which are a good read in their own right, not only for their instructive categories and lists, but also for the restrained accuracy of the descriptive writing.

People

It was only while compiling this text that I appreciated the full extent to which luck and instinct, fuelled by enthusiasm, have guided me through thirty years in the world of gardens.

Nonetheless, without the great understanding and generosity of their owners, I could never have even begun to make the detailed study of those gardens that most interested me and came to influence the garden here.

Not a single person refused me permission or made any restrictions regarding access (it surprised me that they had never had a painter working in their gardens, only photographers). All appreciated the objectivity of my interest—it was the garden that mattered. Furthermore, being themselves

17. Country Life, 1950
18. J. M. Dent & Sons, 1986
19. Joseph Wenman, 1780
20. Harper Collins, 2006
21. Faber and Faber, 1988
22. The Boydell Press, 2002
23. UCP, 2008
24. Black Dog Publishing, 1997
25. Uniformbooks, 2011

creative and professional, they exerted no pressure to produce works subscribing to their own preferences. Once a working routine had been established, I was left to get on.

It is outside the limitations of this publication to give a detailed account of each garden owner; in any case, they and their gardens are already distinguished and celebrated. I hope the following may give some idea of their particular kindness and openhandedness toward me. Anne Dexter gave me the key to her house when she went to Canada for six weeks. Faith Raven, who was away, left food in the fridge and a lovely room to sleep in for a few nights. Beth Chatto gave permission to work in a polytunnel out of the rain, where she kept her special plants. Rosemary Verey, one morning, seeing that the onions in the foreground of a painting had been dug out, silently had them put back by the afternoon. At the Boboli there was no sign of officialdom, just an expressive shrug of the shoulders. Sir Harold Acton never refused me, despite a spate of burglaries, increasingly complex security and, towards the end, failing health. The same courtesy for shorter periods was shown by the directors of the Villa I Tatti (Harvard University) and the Villa le Balze (Georgetown), and the owners of the Villa Gamberaia in Settignano, Villa Medici in Fiesole, and Villa Aldobrandini in Frascati. The botanical gardens at Pisa, Rome, Florence and Padua, although often officially closed during the winter months, always seemed to oblige by leaving a small door open somewhere, and I was never asked to leave. The only risk was to get locked in! At Little Sparta, where I was part of the house-hold, the end room of the cottage became my domain in which to sleep and work. There was always a log fire burning on my arrival and a hot water bottle at night. At Cow Mead Allotments I was the recipient of many kindnesses—the loan of a sun hat, the use of a shed to store my easel and stool, two eggs, garlic and redcurrants…

Opposite page
ABOVE LEFT:
Barnsley House, Kitchen Garden *1984*
ABOVE RIGHT:
Barnsley House, Kitchen Garden, Winter *1986*
BELOW LEFT:
Furzen Leaze Cottages *1985*
BELOW RIGHT:
Little Bowden, Pangbourne, Berkshire *1984*

Page 46:
Villa La Pietra
ABOVE LEFT:
Kitchen Garden with Peppers, *1988*
ABOVE RIGHT:
Apollo & Daphne, *1991*
BELOW LEFT:
Young Bacchus *1989*
BELOW RIGHT:
Kitchen Garden, Marrow and Bougainvillea *1991*

46

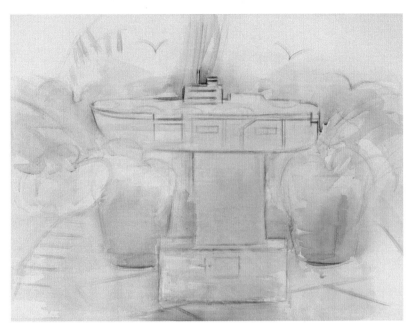

There are so many other people, all good friends to whom I am endebted. Early on in 1985 I met the garden historian, Jane Brown, always a great encourager, who had recently published her groundbreaking book *Gardens of a Golden Afternoon*★. A year later she introduced me to David Wheeler, the gardener and publisher/editor of *Hortus*, through whom I came to know the landscape painter and garden designer, Simon Dorrell. With them I saw many gardens in the UK and Holland and they kept me abreast with much that was happening in the world of gardens and garden literature. The late Norah Byrne arranged a number of weekend trips to see great historic gardens, as well as those listed locally in the NGS *Yellow Book*. The horticultural-ists, Brian and Sue Macdonald of Boxwood Tours and Boxwood Garden Design, were for many happy years my neighbours here in Abingdon. They generously resolved all manner of practicalities in making the garden and introduced me to other professionals from the garden world.

A number of the beautiful interesting gardens I painted early on no longer exist, but of those still thriving in the care of their owners, I am especially thankful to Pauline Trevallion in Siddington, near Cirencester, James and Louise Arbuthnott at Stone House Cottage, near Kidderminster, and the Vereys at little Bowden in Pangbourne. Although no longer at Weobley, Lance and Jane Hattatt at Arrow Cottage were an inspiration. All are passionate gardeners and plant-lovers, infectious in sharing their knowledge and enthusiasms.

★Allen Lane/Penguin Books Ltd, 1982

Coda

In the course of putting together this condensed account of my venture into the world of gardens and gardening, I have been able to enjoy recalling the wonderful variety of beautiful gardens I have visited and painted over a period of thirty years.

But it is those that contained small areas of intensity that I remember with greatest interest and affection. Amongst the most extraordinary are the 'Grotto Di Animali' at the Villa Castello & Petraia in Florence, containing in huge niches three fabulous tableaux of different creatures, from a giraffe to a rabbit, sculpted in dozens of exotic marbles. Another equally entrancing treasure is 'The Rometta' in the south-west corner of the Villa D'Este at Tivoli. It represents an almost childlike vision of Ancient Rome with its miniature temples, sculpture of the she-wolf suckling Romulus and Remus, and a stone boat spouting water, depicting an island in the 'Tiber' and supporting a stone obelisque. These poignant and imaginatively conceived places are matched in my mind to the TV series *Flowering Passions* (HTV West and Channel 4, 1991), written and presented by Anna Pavord, in which she interviews a number of plants-people in less than grand circumstances. Unforgettable were a young radish fancier on a wet and windy allotment overlooking an industrial landscape, a chrysanthemum grower in a miscellany of tattered polytunnels with many of the plants suffering blight, and a plantsman on his highrise balcony in East London, packed with flowers in numerous makeshift containers. In all these kingdoms there was so much to see, inspire and talk about. In each of the gardens I have particularly studied, there existed this same confluence of originality, strength of vision and

19 | 23

compactness. Anne Dexter's tiny shade garden, Rosemary Verey's 'Kitchen Garden', the 'Teatro Verde' at Villa La Pietra, Ian Hamilton Finlay's 'Roman Garden' and John's collection of sheds at the Cow Mead Allotment in Oxford were especially bewitching.

At present I am awaiting the delivery of a book entitled *Transitory Gardens and Uprooted Lives* by Balmori and Morton (YUP 1993). This gives an account of the 'ghetto gardens of the homeless' in New York and shows a black and white photograph of 'Jimmy's Garden', centred on what appears to be a small muddy pool reflecting trees, surrounded by a thoughtfully arranged ensemble of bricks and stones with a trailing fence and the ubiquitous tyres, all overlooked by the creator, relaxing, smoking in a comfortable armchair. Gardens of this type are described as "compositions made in open spaces… which liberate the word 'garden' through their detachment from the usual conditions in which gardens are made". Even though these gardens are very vulnerable, perhaps because they are so vunerable, they serve as a reminder of our instinct and need, regardless of circumstance, to aspire to make something which connects us with the earth.

The impermanent nature of gardens puts them in a category of their own, when seen as works of art. The great gardens of the past and present, and concerns with their conservation/ preservation are important issues of the day. However, no such considerations need trouble the amateur—it is a hobby! In that vein and thinking of the future, although I hope to continue gardening here for some time to come, I do recall an estate agent years ago when viewing the garden, saying expansively "Oh yes! I can just see all this being put down to a nice lawn." Now, admittedly some time later, I can quite happily see what he means.

8

Stinging Nettle and Nasturtium

1. *The Ecology of a Garden: the first fifteen Years*, Jennifer Owen. CUP, 1991

2. *No Nettles Required: the truth about wild life gardening*, Ken Thompson. Eden Project Books, 2006

3. *Baby and Childcare*, Dr Benjamin Spock, 1946

Playing at setting out to attract a wider variety of wildlife in a garden this size could involve all kinds of conflict and compromise. Just recently I have heard about Jennifer Owen's astonishing research project *The Ecology of a Garden* [1] as a result of coming across Ken Thompson's no-nonsense publication *No Nettles Required* [2]. My compulsive reading of this had a similar effect on me as when, in early pregnancy during the 1960s, I was devouring Dr Spock's reassuring commonsense advice on childrearing [3]. In the light of Jennifer Owen's observations on her garden in Leicester and the subsequent research project, 'Biodiversity in Urban Gardens' (BUGS), Thompson expounds in a relaxed and practical way that by just caring for an 'everyday' garden it will inevitably, in the natural order of things, contain a huge quantity of wildlife, whether we like it or not.

Last year, by sparing a handsome stinging nettle (Urtica dioica), the lusty fleet of caterpillars resulting from its attracting a cabbage white butterfly (*Pieris brassicae*), led to the near-disappearance of some climbing nasturtiums close by. I relocated some of them and a few of the flowers and seedheads survived. In the same area, a fine specimen of motherwort (*Leonorus cardiaca*) appeared after the foundations of the garden wall had been dug out, inspiring thoughts of the possible history of this garden and the life of dormant seeds. The less well-tended garden or plot of open ground must surely be seen as an asset in any neighbourhood, as are the splendidly varied wild plants and garden escapees that arrive year after year in the pavements and walls along Spring Road and in the nearby streets. You never know what will appear. Two years ago a single bold colt's-foot (*Tussilago farfara*) with its silver leaves and yellow flowers seeded into the steps up to my front door.

Acknowledgements

At the beginning there were a number of people who made it easier for me to spend so much time in the gardens. I am greatly endebted to Edward Chaney for his introduction to Alta Macadam and Francesco Colacicchi, who for many years lent me their roomy flat at Via Ghibellina in the centre of Florence. During the years at Barnsley, at first I put up in a bed and breakfast in the village, then I stayed as a guest of Davina and Hal Wynne-Jones, and in the last few years I stayed with Charles and Denzil Verey at their cottage in Ampney Crucis. Their kindness and generosity are warmly remembered and appreciated.

In helping me to get started on this publication I am especially grateful to Jessie Sheeler for all her encouragement and interest. Also very many thanks to Jane Brown for her enthusiasm for the idea and invaluable advice on the content of the overall text. I am grateful to Anne de Verteuil and Jess Baines for troubling to read and comment on the introductory paragraphs. Also grateful thanks to Meg Soper, who gave up so much of her time to make this readable with her hours of copy-editing, executed with loving attention to detail.

For the illustrations I have to thank all those owners of paintings, who at some inconvenience to themselves lent them back to be photographed. The reproductions of these works owe much to the skill and patience of Douglas Atfield. Andrew Lawson has, with characteristic kindness, allowed me to reproduce some of the photographs that, over the years, he has taken of the garden here.

The Makers—without whose skill and understanding and patience nothing could ever have been done.

John Andrew: Logo for Tribute to Paul Nash.

Nick Barnard: Table for Tribute to Juan Gris, Umbraumbrae.

Hilary Burns: Basket.

Mike Bury: Postcode.

Laurie Clark: Lettering for Juan Gris.

Fishtail Neon: Gnos.

Joanna Gilmore: Nests for Tribute to Paul Nash and Attenzione!

Nigel Hunter: Handwritten label for Chamomile Lawn.

Nigel Morgan: Wooden eggs for Attenzione!

Redfields Lead Work: River-Bank, This is not an Attack.

John Schofield: Braque/Barque/Baroque, Illi Quinque Gradus, Horizon.

Scorpion Signs: Il Faut Cultiver Notre Jardin, The Allotment Holder, Jardin, Work in Progress, Miscellaneous labelling.

Nick Vincent: Psyché, Poésie, Flower Show, Lawn, Ambulando Solvitur, Faith.

Caroline Webb: Flight, In Memoriam, Hearth, Live Unknown, Q.

Garden Plan on p.36 drawn by Gary Hincks.

Photograph on p.6, and Garden Works nos. 7–10, 16, 25 by Andrew Lawson.

Paintings reproduced are in the collections of Tom & Trish Ayling; Graeme Barrett; Charlbury Dental Practice; Dilys Fleet; Liz Fritsch; Nigel & Stephanie Hunter; John & Ruth Schofield; Charles & Denzil Verey; Joy Whitehead; Isabella Whitworth.